W9-AFY-647

SEP   2009

CHREF
979.3 HAN

Childrens Reference
Does Not Circulate

ELLA JOHNSON MEMORIAL
PUBLIC LIBRARY DISTRICT

109 S. STATE ST.

HAMPSHIRE, IL 60140

(847) 683-4490

DEMCO

THIS LAND CALLED AMERICA: **NEVADA**

CREATIVE EDUCATION

Published by Creative Education
P.O. Box 227, Mankato, Minnesota 56002
Creative Education is an imprint of The Creative Company
www.thecreativecompany.us

Design by Blue Design (www.bluedes.com)
Art direction by Rita Marshall
Book production by The Design Lab
Printed in the United States of America

Photographs by Alamy (ClassicStock, Classic Image, Dale O'Dell, Gistim-
ages, Andrew Hemming, Chuck Nacke, Tom Till), Corbis (Bettmann, David
Muench), Dreamstime (Angeal, Beverett, Photoquest, Tashka), Getty Images
(Clive Brunskill, English School, Ernst Haas, Timothy H. O'Sullivan/George
Eastman House, Frederic Remington, Stephen Toner), iStockphoto (Eric
Foltz, Shaun Lowe, Paul Morton, Laure Neish, Arkady Slavsky), U.S. Air Force
(Master Sgt. Kevin J. Gruenwald)

Copyright © 2010 Creative Education
International copyright reserved in all countries. No part of this book may be
reproduced in any form without written permission from the publisher.

Library of Congress Cataloging-in-Publication Data
Hanel, Rachael.
Nevada / by Rachael Hanel.
p. cm. — (This land called America)
Includes bibliographical references and index.
ISBN 978-1-58341-781-2
1. Nevada—Juvenile literature. I. Title. II. Series.
F841.3.H36 2009
979.3—dc22   2008009510

First Edition
9 8 7 6 5 4 3 2 1

This Land Called America

NEVADA

Rachael Hanel

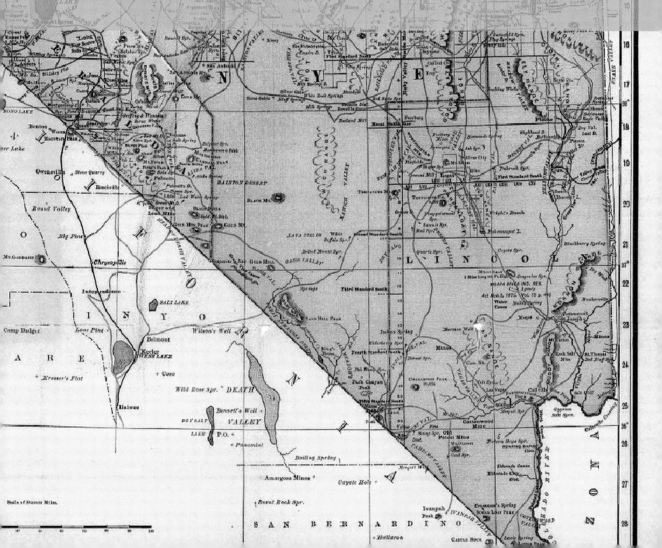

Nevada

RACHAEL HANEL

BRIGHT LIGHTS GLITTER AGAINST THE NIGHT SKY.
MONSTROUS HOTELS RISE LIKE GIANTS FROM THE
DESERT SAND. NOISY CARS CLOG THE STREETS.
PEDESTRIANS CRAM TOGETHER ON SIDEWALKS.
INSIDE HUGE CASINOS, GAMBLERS PLACE THEIR BETS
FOR POKER, BLACKJACK, AND ROULETTE. SINGERS
AND MAGICIANS ENTERTAIN CROWDS GATHERED
IN LARGE THEATERS. VISITORS DINE ON DELICIOUS
MEALS IN FANCY RESTAURANTS. THIS IS THE CITY
OF LAS VEGAS IN SOUTHERN NEVADA. MILLIONS OF
VISITORS COME HERE EACH YEAR FROM ALL AROUND
THE WORLD. THEY STAY UP UNTIL THE WEE HOURS
OF THE MORNING, TRYING TO ENJOY EVERYTHING
THE "ENTERTAINMENT CAPITAL OF THE WORLD"
HAS TO OFFER.

YEAR
1776 Spanish priest Francisco Garcés becomes the first European to travel through Nevada.
EVENT

Gold Rush

Hundreds of years ago, Nevada was a dry, unwelcoming land. Deserts and rugged mountains marked the region. American Indian tribes such as the Paiute, Shoshone, and Washoe adapted to the harshness. They fished in rivers, hunted game such as jackrabbits, and gathered nuts and plants from the land.

Jedediah Smith (above) and other fur traders that followed him became familiar with American Indian tribes such as the Paiute (opposite).

Explorers from Spain claimed much of the southwestern United States, including what is now Nevada, in the 16th century. But they did not settle there. Spanish priest Francisco Garcés' 1776 journey made him the first European to set foot in Nevada. Almost 50 years later, Mexico took control of the area. By the mid-1820s, Canadian and American fur traders such as Peter Skene Ogden and Jedediah Smith were traveling through Nevada to find routes to the Pacific Ocean.

In the 1840s, American mapmaker and explorer John C. Fremont led many expeditions through Nevada. He named

YEAR

1826 Peter Skene Ogden, an explorer and trader for the Hudson's Bay Company, enters northeastern Nevada.

EVENT

- 7 -

it the "Great Basin" because the land was shaped like the bottom of a bowl. Fremont's maps of the area helped others to follow. The first pioneers to settle in Nevada were people who practiced the Mormon religion. Mormons came from the eastern U.S. looking for religious freedom.

Most other pioneers passed through Nevada in covered wagons on their way to California. Pioneers had to cross hundreds of miles of deserts and mountains to get to California. A group called the Donner Party became stuck in snowstorms in the Sierra Nevada mountains of western Nevada in 1846. About half of the almost 90-member party died.

In 1848, Mexico lost the two-year Mexican-American War against the U.S. It signed a peace agreement and gave Nevada to the U.S. Most of Nevada was then included in the Utah Territory, which was established in 1850.

Meanwhile, gold had been discovered in California in 1848. More people traveled through Nevada to get to the gold. A trading post called Mormon Station was founded in 1850 in western Nevada. In 1859, lucky miners struck gold and silver in Nevada. Other mineral deposits were soon discovered, and more towns grew up around the mines.

Once gold or other valuable minerals were found in mines, villages known as "boomtowns" sprang up.

Nevada became a separate territory on March 2, 1861. It became the 36th state on October 31, 1864. After Nevada achieved statehood, more pioneers were lured by the prospect

YEAR

1843 John C. Fremont surveys and begins mapping Nevada, naming the area the "Great Basin."

EVENT

of striking it rich. A railroad was completed through Nevada in 1868. Other railroads soon followed. This made it easier for people to move about the state.

But life was hard for the state's settlers. By 1880, silver prices had dropped, and many mines had dried up. People were left without work or money. Towns were abandoned overnight. Many people left Nevada in search of work.

To help keep people in the state, Nevada passed the State Land Act in 1885. This allowed people to buy land cheaply for $1.25 an acre (0.4 ha). Ranchers raised cattle and sheep in the western and northern parts of the state. Other farmers turned to dairy farming or grew fruit.

The winter of 1889 and 1890 dumped more than 100 inches (254 cm) of snow in the mountain regions. Almost all of the state's ranch animals died. But in 1900, more valuable minerals were discovered. Nevada became home to a second mining wave that once again called many people to the state.

Towns located near railroads, such as Reno (above), grew larger, but those near abandoned mines (opposite) were soon deserted.

YEAR

1848   Mexico gives up land, including present-day Nevada, to the U.S. in the Treaty of Guadalupe Hidalgo.

EVENT

- 10 -

A Dry State

Nevada is the western-most of America's eight Mountain states. It is bordered by Oregon and Idaho to the north. Utah and Arizona are to the east, while California is its neighbor to the west and southwest. In the extreme southeast, a natural boundary is formed by the Colorado River.

Most of Nevada lies within the Great Basin. The mountains in the Great Basin are between 7,000 and 10,000 feet (2,130–3,050 m) high. The basins, or valleys, between the mountains are flat and dry. Some are marked by sand dunes. In other places, the wind has whisked the sand away. What's left behind looks like a floor of rocks. The lowest parts of the basins are called sinks. Water that runs off the mountains sometimes collects in the sinks. The water dries and leaves mud behind. The sun bakes the mud into a hard surface.

In far northeastern Nevada lies part of the Columbia Plateau. This area is marked by lava deposits from old volcanoes that have formed steep canyons. Beyond the canyons, the landscape alternates between flat plains and rolling hills. Western Nevada is covered by the Sierra Nevada mountain range. These mountains are high and steep.

Nevada's Great Basin region is marked by many dry basins (opposite) and is bordered on one end by the Sierra Nevada mountains (above).

YEAR

1851 Genoa and Dayton become the first permanent settlements in Nevada.

EVENT

Several lakes and rivers are found in Nevada. Pyramid Lake and Lake Tahoe are two of the largest bodies of water. They are found in the Sierra Nevada region. In other regions, man-made lakes called reservoirs provide water for drinking and growing crops such as alfalfa, potatoes, and onions.

Nevada shares the Colorado River with its neighbor Arizona. The two states also share the largest man-made lake in the U.S., Lake Mead. Lake Mead was formed when the Hoover Dam was built on the Colorado River in the 1930s. River water backed up behind the dam and formed the lake. Lake Mead supplies water to the nearby city of Las Vegas.

While some lakes, rivers, and reservoirs are used for watering farmland for crops such as potatoes (above), Lake Tahoe (opposite) is used primarily for recreation.

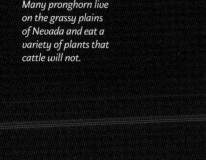
Many pronghorn live on the grassy plains of Nevada and eat a variety of plants that cattle will not.

A pronghorn buck

In Nevada's early days, gold and silver brought great wealth to the state. Nevada is still the largest gold-producing state in America. Other minerals such as iron and copper are mined there, too. Forests of piñon and juniper provide lumber for fences and firewood.

Many animals make their homes in Nevada. Mammals such as rabbits, pronghorn, and elk can be found there. The state's rivers flow with trout and salmon. Game birds include grouse, pheasant, and quail.

Although many people think of Nevada as a hot, dry desert, some parts of the state enjoy mild temperatures and lots of snow. The Sierra Nevada region of western Nevada can receive up to 200 inches (508 cm) of snow a year. But because the high mountains block most rain-bearing clouds that come from the west, much of the rest of Nevada receives little rain. Both the south and the north get only five to eight inches (13–20 cm) of rainfall a year.

In the desert, temperatures can reach well over 100 °F (38 °C) on summer days. But the cloudless, dry climate makes the temperature drop at nightfall. A summer night can be a cool 50 °F (10 °C). At Lake Tahoe, on the western edge of the state, summer highs average 78 °F (26 °C). However, the average high there in January is only 38 °F (3 °C).

Evergreen junipers can grow into tall trees with twisted trunks or spread out as low-lying shrubs.

YEAR
1869   Tracks for the Central Pacific Railroad are completed throughout Nevada.
EVENT

- 17 -

A Growing Population

In the mid-1800s, white settlers in Nevada began taking over land traditionally occupied by American Indians. Many people came to the state hoping to get rich in the gold, silver, and copper mines. Teachers, doctors, and preachers also settled in the towns that sprang up around the

mines. The first settlers included people from the East Coast as well as immigrants from countries such as China, Italy, Germany, and Canada.

A man named Samuel Clemens arrived in Carson City, Nevada, in 1861. His brother was the territorial secretary, and Clemens was looking for adventure. After trying his hand at mining, Clemens began reporting for the *Territorial Enterprise*, a newspaper in Virginia City. There he first used the pen name Mark Twain. As Mark Twain, he became one of America's most famous writers, creating such classic books as *The Adventures of Tom Sawyer* and *The Adventures of Huckleberry Finn*.

Nevada has been home to other notable people who went on to do important work. Thelma Catherine "Pat" Ryan was born in Ely. She married Richard Nixon, who would become the 37th president of the U.S., in 1940. Pat was known for the charitable volunteer work she did as First Lady.

The historic mining town of Virginia City still looks the same today as it did (opposite) when Mark Twain (above) was working there.

YEAR

1911   Las Vegas is incorporated as an official city.

EVENT

Andre Agassi (above) was born in 1970 in Las Vegas, a city famous for its bright lights and big buildings (opposite).

Tennis superstar Andre Agassi is from Nevada, too. He won eight Grand Slam tennis titles and an Olympic gold medal. He formed a charity in 1994 to help at-risk children in southern Nevada. Agassi is married to another tennis star, Steffi Graf. They live in Agassi's hometown of Las Vegas.

Nevada is a diverse state. White people make up just over half of the state's population. About 25 percent of Nevadans are Latino. African Americans, American Indians, and Asian Americans make up smaller percentages of Nevada's population.

Nevada's large population of Latinos influences the state in many ways. National politicians pay attention to the state's Latino voters and what they have to say. And Mexican restaurants around the state are popular for their foods such as tacos, enchiladas, and fajitas.

Sixteen percent of Nevada's population was born in another country, such as Mexico. Many immigrants come looking for jobs in the tourism industry. Tourism and gambling are Nevada's largest industries. Taxes collected from gambling supply Nevada's government with lots of money. The cities

1931 Construction begins on the Hoover Dam, the highest dam of its kind in the U.S.

Huge trucks that can carry 100-ton (91 t) loads are used to remove gold from mines in Nevada.

of Las Vegas and Reno need many people to work in their busy hotels and restaurants and to provide transportation. One out of every 10 Nevadans is employed by the hotel and food industries.

Today, mining also remains an important industry in Nevada. The state ranks second in the nation in mineral production. Nevada's mines produce gold, crushed stone, and silver. The state is a leading producer of electricity as well, thanks to the energy produced by the Hoover Dam. Electricity from Nevada is sent hundreds of miles away to places such as Los Angeles, California.

The 726-foot-high (221 m) Hoover Dam was built between 1931 and 1936 in Black Canyon.

YEAR

1931   Nevada becomes the first state to legalize gambling.

EVENT

Nevada ranch

N evada was the fastest-growing state from 1990 to 2000. In that time, its population increased from 1.2 million to nearly 2 million. Most newcomers settled in the southern and western parts of the state.

Outside of Las Vegas, the state is thinly populated. In the eastern part of Nevada, travelers can drive miles without seeing a house. On average, there are only 21.3 people per square mile (2.6 sq km). There's plenty of room to spread out in Nevada.

Much of the land not used for farming or ranching (above) is owned by the U.S. government for the purpose of conducting dangerous tests (opposite).

YEARS
1951 Atomic bomb testing begins in the Nevada desert.
EVENT

A Sense of Community

Millions of people visit Nevada each year. Many of them travel to Las Vegas. A century ago, the city consisted of nothing more than a few shacks. Now Las Vegas is crowded with dozens of casinos and more than 150,000 hotel rooms. Some people like to gamble in Las Vegas, but there are other

things to do there as well. Families shop and go to magic shows and musical performances.

Visitors looking for more peace and quiet can travel Highway 50. This roughly 300-mile-long (483 km) road is called the "Loneliest Road in America." It spans the width of the state, following an old Pony Express route. Mountain ranges, frontier cemeteries, and ghost towns make the trip interesting.

Ghost towns were once thriving mining towns, but when all the minerals had been extracted from a mine, the towns closed almost overnight. Houses, churches, and hotels were abandoned as miners moved on in search of new, untapped mines. Now, only visitors walk the dusty streets of these towns.

Nevada's ghost towns may be deserted, but other attractions around the state are full of life. Resorts in the Sierra Nevadas are popular destinations for skiers. Other visitors relax on the scenic shores of Lake Tahoe. Some people like to explore the state's many parks.

Nevada welcomes tourists who visit its exciting cities such as Las Vegas (opposite) as well as its historical ghost towns (above).

YEAR

1978 The U.S. government begins studying Yucca Mountain as a possible site for disposing of nuclear waste.

EVENT

One of the most amazing man-made structures in Nevada is the Hoover Dam. More than 21,000 people worked on the enormous concrete dam, which was finished in 1936. Water from the Colorado River flows through the dam to generate electricity.

The federal government owns 80 percent of Nevada's land. It owns more land there than in any other state. The government's land includes national parks, forests, and military bases. Nevada's solitude makes it an ideal location for a top-secret Air Force base known as "Area 51." It's located in southern Nevada. Because Area 51 is so secret, people come up with many theories about what goes on there. Many people think this is where new aircraft are tested. Enemy aircraft may also be studied there. Some people even think that crashed UFOs are taken there to be examined.

Nevada plays important roles in producing energy (through the Hoover Dam, above) and in providing space for military exercises (opposite).

QUICK FACTS

Population: 2,565,382

Largest city: Las Vegas (pop. 558,880)

Capital: Carson City

Entered the union: October 31, 1864

Nickname: Sagebrush State

State flower: sagebrush

State bird: mountain bluebird

Size: 110,561 square miles (286,352 sq km)—7th-biggest in U.S.

Major industries: tourism, mining, agriculture

Nevada was an important site for nuclear bomb tests in the 1950s. The U.S. needed a remote spot to test these powerful new weapons. Although nuclear testing officially ended there in 1992, visitors can learn more about this time in history at the Atomic Testing Museum in Las Vegas.

For entertainment, Nevadans like to attend sporting events. Nevada does not have any professional sports teams. Instead, people root for sports programs at the University of Nevada–Las Vegas. Golf, rodeos, and NASCAR racing are also popular sports there. Each year, the Las Vegas Motor Speedway hosts the UAW-Dodge 400.

Nevada is a state filled with contrasts. Even while much of the state remains empty, bigger and grander hotels are planned for Las Vegas. With more tourists coming in, more people will be needed to live and work in the state, so Nevada's growth is unlikely to slow down any time soon. Whether people are looking for the fast pace of city life or the quiet solitude of wilderness, there's something to suit everyone in Nevada.

YEAR

2007　American adventurer Steve Fossett goes missing while on a flight over the western Nevada desert.

EVENT

- 31 -

BIBLIOGRAPHY

Bowers, Michael W. *The Sagebrush State: Nevada's History, Government, & Politics.* Reno, Nev.: University of Nevada Press, 1996.

Laxalt, Robert. *Nevada: A Bicentennial History.* New York: W. W. Norton, 1977.

Nevada History. "Homepage: A Walk in the Past." Nevada-History.org. http://nevada-history.org.

Reid, John B., and Ronald M. James. *Uncovering Nevada's Past: A Primary Source History of the Silver State.* Reno, Nev.: University of Nevada Press, 2004.

Worldmark Encyclopedia of the States. Vol. 2. Detroit: Thomson Gale, 2007.

INDEX